This Book

Belongs to

_____

_____

_____

2022

January
S	M	T	W	T	F	S
						1
2	3	4	5	6	7	8
9	10	11	12	13	14	15
16	(17)	18	19	20	21	22
23	24	25	26	27	28	29
30	31					

February
S	M	T	W	T	F	S
		1	2	3	4	5
6	7	8	9	10	11	12
13	14	15	16	17	18	19
20	(21)	22	23	24	25	26
27	28					

March
S	M	T	W	T	F	S
		1	2	3	4	5
6	7	8	9	10	11	12
13	14	15	16	17	18	19
20	21	22	23	24	25	26
27	28	29	30	31		

April
S	M	T	W	T	F	S
					1	2
3	4	5	6	7	8	9
10	11	12	13	14	15	16
17	18	19	20	21	22	23
24	25	26	27	28	29	30

May
S	M	T	W	T	F	S
1	2	3	4	5	6	7
8	9	10	11	12	13	14
15	16	17	18	19	20	21
22	23	24	25	26	27	28
29	(30)	31				

June
S	M	T	W	T	F	S
			1	2	3	4
5	6	7	8	9	10	11
12	13	14	15	16	17	18
19	(20)	21	22	23	24	25
26	27	28	29	30		

July
S	M	T	W	T	F	S
					1	2
3	(4)	5	6	7	8	9
10	11	12	13	14	15	16
17	18	19	20	21	22	23
24	25	26	27	28	29	30
31						

August
S	M	T	W	T	F	S
	1	2	3	4	5	6
7	8	9	10	11	12	13
14	15	16	17	18	19	20
21	22	23	24	25	26	27
28	29	30	31			

September
S	M	T	W	T	F	S
				1	2	3
4	(5)	6	7	8	9	10
11	12	13	14	15	16	17
18	19	20	21	22	23	24
25	26	27	28	29	30	

October
S	M	T	W	T	F	S
						1
2	3	4	5	6	7	8
9	(10)	11	12	13	14	15
16	17	18	19	20	21	22
23	24	25	26	27	28	29
30	31					

November
S	M	T	W	T	F	S
		1	2	3	4	5
6	7	8	9	10	11	12
13	14	15	16	17	18	19
20	21	22	23	24	25	26
27	28	29	30			

December
S	M	T	W	T	F	S
				1	2	3
4	5	6	7	8	9	10
11	12	13	14	15	16	17
18	19	20	21	22	23	24
25	(26)	27	28	29	30	31

Jan 1	● New Year's Day	May 8	● Mother's Day	Oct 31	● Halloween
Jan 17	● Martin Luther King Jr. Day	May 30	● Memorial Day	Nov 8	● Election Day
Feb 14	● Valentine's Day	Jun 14	● Flag Day	Nov 11	● Veterans Day
Feb 21	● Presidents' Day	Jun 19	● Father's Day	Nov 24	● Thanksgiving Day
Mar 17	● St. Patrick's Day	Jun 19	● Juneteenth	Nov 25	● Black Friday
Apr 17	● Easter Sunday	Jun 20	● 'Juneteenth' day off	Dec 24	● Christmas Eve
Apr 18	● Easter Monday	Jul 4	● Independence Day	Dec 25	● Christmas Day
Apr 18	● Tax Day	Sep 5	● Labor Day	Dec 26	● 'Christmas Day' day off
May 5	● Cinco de Mayo	Oct 10	● Columbus Day	Dec 31	● New Year's Eve

Jan 2022

Sunday	Monday	Tuesday	Wednesday	Thursday	Friday	Saturday
						1
2	3	4	5	6	7	8
9	10	11	12	13	14	15
16	17	18	19	20	21	22
23	24	25	26	27	28	29
30	31					

February

S	M	T	W	T	F	S
		1	2	3	4	5
6	7	8	9	10	11	12
13	14	15	16	17	18	19
20	(21)	22	23	24	25	26
27	28					

Top Priorities

Important

Birthdays -Anniversaries

Notes

More of

1

2

To Do

- [ ]
- [ ]
- [ ]
- [ ]
- [ ]
- [ ]
- [ ]
- [ ]
- [ ]
- [ ]
- [ ]

Less of

Income

Date	Description	Amount

Expense

Housing	Amount

Shoping	Amount

Total Income	Total Outgoing	Balance

Note

Feb 2022

Sunday	Monday	Tuesday	Wednesday	Thursday	Friday	Saturday
		1	2	3	4	5
6	7	8	9	10	11	12
13	14	15	16	17	18	19
20	21	22	23	24	25	26
27	28					

March

S	M	T	W	T	F	S
		1	2	3	4	5
6	7	8	9	10	11	12
13	14	15	16	17	18	19
20	21	22	23	24	25	26
27	28	29	30	31		

Top Priorities

Important

....
....
....
....
....
_____

Birthdays -Anniversaries

....
....
....
....
....
_____

Notes

....
....
....
....
....
....
....
....
....
....
....
_____

More of

....
....
....
....
....
_____

1

2

To Do

- ☐
- ☐
- ☐
- ☐
- ☐
- ☐
- ☐
- ☐
- ☐
- ☐
- ☐
_____

Less of

....
....
....
....
....
_____

Income

Date	Description	Amount

Expense

Housing	Amount

Shoping	Amount

Total Income	Total Outgoing	Balance

Note

March 2022

Sunday	Monday	Tuesday	Wednesday	Thursday	Friday	Saturday
		1	2	3	4	5
6	7	8	9	10	11	12
13	14	15	16	17	18	19
20	21	22	23	24	25	26
27	28	29	30	31		

April

S	M	T	W	T	F	S
					1	2
3	4	5	6	7	8	9
10	11	12	13	14	15	16
17	18	19	20	21	22	23
24	25	26	27	28	29	30

Top Priorities

Important

1

Birthdays -Anniversaries

2

Notes

To Do

- [ ]
- [ ]
- [ ]
- [ ]
- [ ]
- [ ]
- [ ]
- [ ]
- [ ]
- [ ]
- [ ]

More of

Less of

Income

Date	Description	Amount

Expense

Housing	Amount

Shoping	Amount

Total Income	Total Outgoing	Balance

Note

April 2022

Sunday	Monday	Tuesday	Wednesday	Thursday	Friday	Saturday
					1	2
3	4	5	6	7	8	9
10	11	12	13	14	15	16
17	18	19	20	21	22	23
24	25	26	27	28	29	30

May

S	M	T	W	T	F	S
1	2	3	4	5	6	7
8	9	10	11	12	13	14
15	16	17	18	19	20	21
22	23	24	25	26	27	28
29	(30)	31				

Top Priorities

Important

Birthdays -Anniversaries

Notes

More of

1

2

To Do

- [ ]
- [ ]
- [ ]
- [ ]
- [ ]
- [ ]
- [ ]
- [ ]
- [ ]
- [ ]
- [ ]

Less of

Income

Date	Description	Amount

Expense

Housing	Amount

Shoping	Amount

Total Income	Total Outgoing	Balance

May 2022

Sunday	Monday	Tuesday	Wednesday	Thursday	Friday	Saturday
1	2	3	4	5	6	7
8	9	10	11	12	13	14
15	16	17	18	19	20	21
22	23	24	25	26	27	28
29	30	31				

June

S	M	T	W	T	F	S
			1	2	3	4
5	6	7	8	9	10	11
12	13	14	15	16	17	18
19	(20)	21	22	23	24	25
26	27	28	29	30		

Top Priorities

Important

....
....
....
....
....
....

1

Birthdays -Anniversaries

....
....
....
....
....

2

Notes

....
....
....
....
....
....
....
....
....
....

To Do

☐ ....
☐ ....
☐ ....
☐ ....
☐ ....
☐ ....
☐ ....
☐ ....
☐ ....
☐ ....
☐ ....

More of

....
....
....
....
....
....

Less of

....
....
....
....
....
....

Income

Date	Description	Amount

Expense

Housing	Amount

Shoping	Amount

Total Income	Total Outgoing	Balance

Jun 2022

Sunday	Monday	Tuesday	Wednesday	Thursday	Friday	Saturday
			1	2	3	4
5	6	7	8	9	10	11
12	13	14	15	16	17	18
19	20	21	22	23	24	25
26	27	28	29	30		

July

S	M	T	W	T	F	S
					1	2
3	4	5	6	7	8	9
10	11	12	13	14	15	16
17	18	19	20	21	22	23
24	25	26	27	28	29	30
31						

Top Priorities

Important

....
....
....
....
....

Birthdays -Anniversaries

....
....
....
....
....

Notes

....
....
....
....
....
....
....
....
....
....
....
....

More of

....
....
....
....
....
....

1

2

To Do

- ☐ ....
- ☐ ....
- ☐ ....
- ☐ ....
- ☐ ....
- ☐ ....
- ☐ ....
- ☐ ....
- ☐ ....
- ☐ ....
- ☐ ....

Less of

....
....
....
....
....
....

Income

Date	Description	Amount

Expense

Housing	Amount

Shoping	Amount

Total Income	Total Outgoing	Balance

Note

July 2022

Sunday	Monday	Tuesday	Wednesday	Thursday	Friday	Saturday
					1	2
3	4	5	6	7	8	9
10	11	12	13	14	15	16
17	18	19	20	21	22	23
24	25	26	27	28	29	30
31						

August

S	M	T	W	T	F	S
	1	2	3	4	5	6
7	8	9	10	11	12	13
14	15	16	17	18	19	20
21	22	23	24	25	26	27
28	29	30	31			

Top Priorities

Important

Birthdays -Anniversaries

Notes

More of

1

2

To Do

- [ ]
- [ ]
- [ ]
- [ ]
- [ ]
- [ ]
- [ ]
- [ ]
- [ ]
- [ ]
- [ ]

Less of

Income

Date	Description	Amount

Expense

Housing	Amount

Shoping	Amount

Total Income	Total Outgoing	Balance

Note

August 2022

Sunday	Monday	Tuesday	Wednesday	Thursday	Friday	Saturday
	1	2	3	4	5	6
7	8	9	10	11	12	13
14	15	16	17	18	19	20
21	22	23	24	25	26	27
28	29	30	31			

September

S	M	T	W	T	F	S
				1	2	3
4	5	6	7	8	9	10
11	12	13	14	15	16	17
18	19	20	21	22	23	24
25	26	27	28	29	30	

Top Priorities

Important

Birthdays -Anniversaries

Notes

More of

1

2

To Do

- [ ]
- [ ]
- [ ]
- [ ]
- [ ]
- [ ]
- [ ]
- [ ]
- [ ]
- [ ]
- [ ]

Less of

Income

Date	Description	Amount

Expense

Housing	Amount

Shoping	Amount

Total Income	Total Outgoing	Balance

Note

September 2022

Sunday	Monday	Tuesday	Wednesday	Thursday	Friday	Saturday
				1	2	3
4	5	6	7	8	9	10
11	12	13	14	15	16	17
18	19	20	21	22	23	24
25	26	27	28	29	30	

October

S	M	T	W	T	F	S
						1
2	3	4	5	6	7	8
9	10	11	12	13	14	15
16	17	18	19	20	21	22
23	24	25	26	27	28	29
30	31					

Top Priorities

Important

Birthdays -Anniversaries

Notes

1

2

To Do

- [ ]
- [ ]
- [ ]
- [ ]
- [ ]
- [ ]
- [ ]
- [ ]
- [ ]
- [ ]
- [ ]

More of

Less of

Income

Date	Description	Amount

Expense

Housing	Amount

Shoping	Amount

Total Income	Total Outgoing	Balance

Note

October 2022

Sunday	Monday	Tuesday	Wednesday	Thursday	Friday	Saturday
						1
2	3	4	5	6	7	8
9	10	11	12	13	14	15
16	17	18	19	20	21	22
23	24	25	26	27	28	29
30	31					

November

S	M	T	W	T	F	S
		1	2	3	4	5
6	7	8	9	10	11	12
13	14	15	16	17	18	19
20	21	22	23	24	25	26
27	28	29	30			

Top Priorities

Important

Birthdays -Anniversaries

Notes

More of

1

2

To Do

- [ ]
- [ ]
- [ ]
- [ ]
- [ ]
- [ ]
- [ ]
- [ ]
- [ ]
- [ ]
- [ ]

Less of

Income

Date	Description	Amount

Expense

Housing	Amount

Shoping	Amount

Total Income	Total Outgoing	Balance

Note

November 2022

Sunday	Monday	Tuesday	Wednesday	Thursday	Friday	Saturday
		1	2	3	4	5
6	7	8	9	10	11	12
13	14	15	16	17	18	19
20	21	22	23	24	25	26
27	28	29	30			

December

S	M	T	W	T	F	S
				1	2	3
4	5	6	7	8	9	10
11	12	13	14	15	16	17
18	19	20	21	22	23	24
25	(26)	27	28	29	30	31

Top Priorities

Important

Birthdays -Anniversaries

Notes

More of

1

2

To Do
- ☐
- ☐
- ☐
- ☐
- ☐
- ☐
- ☐
- ☐
- ☐
- ☐
- ☐

Less of

Income

Date	Description	Amount

Expense

Housing	Amount

Shoping	Amount

Total Income	Total Outgoing	Balance

Note

December 2022

Sunday	Monday	Tuesday	Wednesday	Thursday	Friday	Saturday
				1	2	3
4	5	6	7	8	9	10
11	12	13	14	15	16	17
18	19	20	21	22	23	24
25	26	27	28	29	30	31

Top Priorities

Important

....
....
....
....
....
....

Birthdays -Anniversaries

....
....
....
....
....

Notes

....
....
....
....
....
....
....
....
....
....
....

More of

....
....
....
....
....
....
....
....

1

2

To Do

- ☐
- ☐
- ☐
- ☐
- ☐
- ☐
- ☐
- ☐
- ☐
- ☐
- ☐

Less of

....
....
....
....
....
....
....
....

Income

Date	Description	Amount

Expense

Housing	Amount

Shoping	Amount

Total Income	Total Outgoing	Balance

Note

Websites & Passwords

Website

Username:
E-mail:
Password:

Website

Username:
E-mail:
Password:

Website

Username:
E-mail:
Password:

Website

Username:
E-mail:
Password:

Website

Username:
E-mail:
Password:

Website

Username:
E-mail:
Password:

Website

Username:
E-mail:
Password:

Website

Username:
E-mail:
Password:

Website

Username:
E-mail:
Password:

Website

Username:
E-mail:
Password:

Website

Username:
E-mail:
Password:

Website

Username:
E-mail:
Password:

Website

Username:
E-mail:
Password:

Website

Username:
E-mail:
Password:

Websites & Passwords

Website

Username:
E-mail:
Password:

Website

Username:
E-mail:
Password:

Website

Username:
E-mail:
Password:

Website

Username:
E-mail:
Password:

Website

Username:
E-mail:
Password:

Website

Username:
E-mail:
Password:

Website

Username:
E-mail:
Password:

Website

Username:
E-mail:
Password:

Website

Username:
E-mail:
Password:

Website

Username:
E-mail:
Password:

Website

Username:
E-mail:
Password:

Website

Username:
E-mail:
Password:

Website

Username:
E-mail:
Password:

Website

Username:
E-mail:
Password:

Websites & Passwords

Website

Username:
E-mail:
Password:

Website

Username:
E-mail:
Password:

Website

Username:
E-mail:
Password:

Website

Username:
E-mail:
Password:

Website

Username:
E-mail:
Password:

Website

Username:
E-mail:
Password:

Website

Username:
E-mail:
Password:

Website

Username:
E-mail:
Password:

Website

Username:
E-mail:
Password:

Website

Username:
E-mail:
Password:

Website

Username:
E-mail:
Password:

Website

Username:
E-mail:
Password:

Website

Username:
E-mail:
Password:

Website

Username:
E-mail:
Password:

Books to Read List

Title	Author	Genre	Rating
			☆☆☆☆☆
			☆☆☆☆☆
			☆☆☆☆☆
			☆☆☆☆☆
			☆☆☆☆☆
			☆☆☆☆☆
			☆☆☆☆☆
			☆☆☆☆☆
			☆☆☆☆☆
			☆☆☆☆☆
			☆☆☆☆☆
			☆☆☆☆☆
			☆☆☆☆☆
			☆☆☆☆☆
			☆☆☆☆☆
			☆☆☆☆☆
			☆☆☆☆☆
			☆☆☆☆☆
			☆☆☆☆☆
			☆☆☆☆☆
			☆☆☆☆☆
			☆☆☆☆☆
			☆☆☆☆☆

Books to Read List

Title	Author	Genre	Rating
			☆☆☆☆☆
			☆☆☆☆☆
			☆☆☆☆☆
			☆☆☆☆☆
			☆☆☆☆☆
			☆☆☆☆☆
			☆☆☆☆☆
			☆☆☆☆☆
			☆☆☆☆☆
			☆☆☆☆☆
			☆☆☆☆☆
			☆☆☆☆☆
			☆☆☆☆☆
			☆☆☆☆☆
			☆☆☆☆☆
			☆☆☆☆☆
			☆☆☆☆☆
			☆☆☆☆☆
			☆☆☆☆☆
			☆☆☆☆☆
			☆☆☆☆☆
			☆☆☆☆☆
			☆☆☆☆☆
			☆☆☆☆☆

Books to Read List

Title	Author	Genre	Rating
			☆☆☆☆☆
			☆☆☆☆☆
			☆☆☆☆☆
			☆☆☆☆☆
			☆☆☆☆☆
			☆☆☆☆☆
			☆☆☆☆☆
			☆☆☆☆☆
			☆☆☆☆☆
			☆☆☆☆☆
			☆☆☆☆☆
			☆☆☆☆☆
			☆☆☆☆☆
			☆☆☆☆☆
			☆☆☆☆☆
			☆☆☆☆☆
			☆☆☆☆☆
			☆☆☆☆☆
			☆☆☆☆☆
			☆☆☆☆☆
			☆☆☆☆☆
			☆☆☆☆☆
			☆☆☆☆☆
			☆☆☆☆☆

Movies List

Name:	Name:
Rating:	Rating:

Name:	Name:
Rating:	Rating:

Name:	Name:
Rating:	Rating:

Name:	Name:
Rating:	Rating:

Name:	Name:
Rating:	Rating:

Name:	Name:
Rating:	Rating:

Name:	Name:
Rating:	Rating:

Name:	Name:
Rating:	Rating:

Name:	Name:
Rating:	Rating:

Movies List

Name:
Rating:

Name:
Rating:

Name:
Rating:

Name:
Rating:

Name:
Rating:

Name:
Rating:

Name:
Rating:

Name:
Rating:

Name:
Rating:

Name:
Rating:

Name:
Rating:

Name:
Rating:

Name:
Rating:

Name:
Rating:

Name:
Rating:

Name:
Rating:

Name:
Rating:

Name:
Rating:

Sries List

Name:		Name:
Rating:		Rating:

Name:		Name:
Rating:		Rating:

Name:		Name:
Rating:		Rating:

Name:		Name:
Rating:		Rating:

Name:		Name:
Rating:		Rating:

Name:		Name:
Rating:		Rating:

Name:		Name:
Rating:		Rating:

Name:		Name:
Rating:		Rating:

Name:		Name:
Rating:		Rating:

Sries List

Name:	Name:
Rating:	Rating:

Name:	Name:
Rating:	Rating:

Name:	Name:
Rating:	Rating:

Name:	Name:
Rating:	Rating:

Name:	Name:
Rating:	Rating:

Name:	Name:
Rating:	Rating:

Name:	Name:
Rating:	Rating:

Name:	Name:
Rating:	Rating:

Name:	Name:
Rating:	Rating:

Year at A Glance

JANUARY

FEBRUARY

MARCH

APRIL

MAY

JUNE

Year at A Glance

JANUARY

FEBRUARY

MARCH

APRIL

MAY

JUNE

369
Manifestation Journal

Turn your life upside down for the better...
With the power of 369.

But how...they are nothing but numbers. Indeed they are.
But they are not just any numbers. They are sacred.
They hold the secret of the Universe. As Tesla once said:

"If you only knew the magnificence of the 3, 6 and 9,
then you would have the key to the universe."

No matter how you divide a circle you'll always end up with

3,6 or 9.

No matter how many times you've divided 1, the outcome is

3,6 or 9.

Our cells get multiplied from 1 to 2, then 4, 8, 16(1+6=7), 32(3+2 = 5),
64(6+4 =10(which is again 1)), ...etc.,
If you look the entire series it will give you the pattern like
1,2,4,8,7,5,1,2,4,8,7......etc... The mysterious part is,
if you continue with this, you'll never find the three numbers 3, 6 and 9.
They're beyond this pattern.

How to use this journal?

Follow these steps:

1. Think really hard of what you EXACTLY want from the Universe. Hold that thought for at least 17 seconds. This is for getting momentum.

2. Write down your desire three times in the morning. Then just let go. This is the way you tell the Universe: "I trust you".

3. Through the day, write it down six more times. Visualize to and feel it as if you already have it.

4. At night, before bedtime, write it down nine times. This will get into your subconscious and start manifesting in your dreams first.
5. Thank the Universe.

6. Repeat for 33 up to 45 days.

Be specific with your wish!
Trust the process!
Be honestly thankful!

Date:_____/_____/_____

Morning

1. _____
_____
2. _____
_____
3. _____
_____

Afternoon

1. _____
_____
2. _____
_____
3. _____
_____
4 _____
_____
5. _____
_____
6. _____
_____

I unleash my desire with love, trust and gratefulness.

Date:_____/_____/_____

Evening

1. _____
   _____

2. _____
   _____

3. _____
   _____

4 _____
   _____

5. _____
   _____

6. _____
   _____

7 _____
   _____

8. _____
   _____

9. _____
   _____

I unleash my desire with love, trust and gratefulness.

Date:_____/_____/_____

Morning

1. _____
   _____
2. _____
   _____
3. _____
   _____

Afternoon

1. _____
   _____
2. _____
   _____
3. _____
   _____
4 _____
   _____
5. _____
   _____
6. _____
   _____

I unleash my desire with love, trust and gratefulness.

Date:_____/_____/_____

Evening

1. _____

2. _____

3. _____

4 _____

5. _____

6. _____

7 _____

8. _____

9. _____

I unleash my desire with love, trust and gratefulness.

Date:_____/_____/_____

Morning

1. _____
_____
2. _____
_____
3. _____
_____

Afternoon

1. _____
_____
2. _____
_____
3. _____
_____
4 _____
_____
5. _____
_____
6. _____
_____

I unleash my desire with love, trust and gratefulness.

Date:_____/_____/_____

Evening

1. _____
   _____
2. _____
   _____
3. _____
   _____
4 _____
   _____
5. _____
   _____
6. _____
   _____
7 _____
   _____
8. _____
   _____
9. _____
   _____

I unleash my desire with love, trust and gratefulness.

Date:_____/_____/_____

Morning

1. _____
   _____
2. _____
   _____
3. _____
   _____

Afternoon

1. _____
   _____
2. _____
   _____
3. _____
   _____
4 _____
   _____
5. _____
   _____
6. _____
   _____

I unleash my desire with love, trust and gratefulness.

Date:_____/_____/_____

Evening

1. _____
   _____
2. _____
   _____
3. _____
   _____
4 _____
   _____
5. _____
   _____
6. _____
   _____
7 _____
   _____
8. _____
   _____
9. _____
   _____

I unleash my desire with love, trust and gratefulness.

Date:_____/_____/_____

Morning

1. _____
   _____
2. _____
   _____
3. _____
   _____

Afternoon

1. _____
   _____
2. _____
   _____
3. _____
   _____
4 _____
   _____
5. _____
   _____
6. _____
   _____

I unleash my desire with love, trust and gratefulness.

Date:_____/_____/_____

Evening

1. _____
_____

2. _____
_____

3. _____
_____

4 _____
_____

5. _____
_____

6. _____
_____

7 _____
_____

8. _____
_____

9. _____
_____

I unleash my desire with love, trust and gratefulness.

Date:_____/_____/_____

Morning

1. _____
   _____
2. _____
   _____
3. _____
   _____

Afternoon

1. _____
   _____
2. _____
   _____
3. _____
   _____
4. _____
   _____
5. _____
   _____
6. _____
   _____

I unleash my desire with love, trust and gratefulness.

Date:_____/_____/_____

Evening

1. _____
   _____
2. _____
   _____
3. _____
   _____
4. _____
   _____
5. _____
   _____
6. _____
   _____
7. _____
   _____
8. _____
   _____
9. _____
   _____

I unleash my desire with love, trust and gratefulness.

Date:_____/_____/_____

Morning

1. _____
   _____
2. _____
   _____
3. _____
   _____

Afternoon

1. _____
   _____
2. _____
   _____
3. _____
   _____
4 _____
   _____
5. _____
   _____
6. _____
   _____

I unleash my desire with love, trust and gratefulness.

Date:_____/_____/_____

Evening

1. _____
_____

2. _____
_____

3. _____
_____

4 _____
_____

5. _____
_____

6. _____
_____

7 _____
_____

8. _____
_____

9. _____
_____

I unleash my desire with love, trust and gratefulness.

Date:_____/_____/_____

Morning

1. _____
   _____
2. _____
   _____
3. _____
   _____

Afternoon

1. _____
   _____
2. _____
   _____
3. _____
   _____
4 _____
   _____
5. _____
   _____
6. _____
   _____

I unleash my desire with love, trust and gratefulness.

Date:_____/_____/_____

Evening

1. _____
_____

2. _____
_____

3. _____
_____

4 _____
_____

5. _____
_____

6. _____
_____

7 _____
_____

8. _____
_____

9. _____
_____

I unleash my desire with love, trust and gratefulness.

Date:_____/_____/_____

Morning

1. _____
   _____
2. _____
   _____
3. _____
   _____

Afternoon

1. _____
   _____
2. _____
   _____
3. _____
   _____
4 _____
   _____
5. _____
   _____
6. _____
   _____

I unleash my desire with love, trust and gratefulness.

Date:_____/_____/_____

Evening

1. _____
   _____
2. _____
   _____
3. _____
   _____
4 _____
   _____
5. _____
   _____
6. _____
   _____
7 _____
   _____
8. _____
   _____
9. _____
   _____

I unleash my desire with love, trust and gratefulness.

Date:_____/_____/_____

Morning

1. _____
   _____
2. _____
   _____
3. _____
   _____

Afternoon

1. _____
   _____
2. _____
   _____
3. _____
   _____
4 _____
   _____
5. _____
   _____
6. _____
   _____

I unleash my desire with love, trust and gratefulness.

Date:_____/_____/_____

Evening

1. _____
   _____

2. _____
   _____

3. _____
   _____

4 _____
   _____

5. _____
   _____

6. _____
   _____

7 _____
   _____

8. _____
   _____

9. _____
   _____

I unleash my desire with love, trust and gratefulness.

Date:_____/_____/_____

Morning

1. _____
   _____
2. _____
   _____
3. _____
   _____

Afternoon

1. _____
   _____
2. _____
   _____
3. _____
   _____
4. _____
   _____
5. _____
   _____
6. _____
   _____

I unleash my desire with love, trust and gratefulness.

Date:_____/_____/_____

Evening

1. _____
   _____

2. _____
   _____

3. _____
   _____

4 _____
   _____

5. _____
   _____

6. _____
   _____

7 _____
   _____

8. _____
   _____

9. _____
   _____

I unleash my desire with love, trust and gratefulness.

Date:_____/_____/_____

Morning

1. _____
   _____
2. _____
   _____
3. _____
   _____

Afternoon

1. _____
   _____
2. _____
   _____
3. _____
   _____
4 _____
   _____
5. _____
   _____
6. _____
   _____

I unleash my desire with love, trust and gratefulness.

Date:_____/_____/_____

Evening

1. _____
   _____
2. _____
   _____
3. _____
   _____
4 _____
   _____
5. _____
   _____
6. _____
   _____
7 _____
   _____
8. _____
   _____
9. _____
   _____

I unleash my desire with love, trust and gratefulness.

Date:_____/_____/_____

Morning

1. _____
   _____
2. _____
   _____
3. _____
   _____

Afternoon

1. _____
   _____
2. _____
   _____
3. _____
   _____
4 _____
   _____
5. _____
   _____
6. _____
   _____

I unleash my desire with love, trust and gratefulness.

Date:_____/_____/_____

Evening

1. _____
   _____
2. _____
   _____
3. _____
   _____
4 _____
   _____
5. _____
   _____
6. _____
   _____
7 _____
   _____
8. _____
   _____
9. _____
   _____

I unleash my desire with love, trust and gratefulness.

Date:_____/_____/_____

Morning

1. _____
   _____
2. _____
   _____
3. _____
   _____

Afternoon

1. _____
   _____
2. _____
   _____
3. _____
   _____
4 _____
   _____
5. _____
   _____
6. _____
   _____

I unleash my desire with love, trust and gratefulness.

Date:_____/_____/_____

Evening

1. _____
_____

2. _____
_____

3. _____
_____

4 _____
_____

5. _____
_____

6. _____
_____

7 _____
_____

8. _____
_____

9. _____
_____

I unleash my desire with love, trust and gratefulness.

Date:_____/_____/_____

Morning

1. _____
   _____
2. _____
   _____
3. _____
   _____

Afternoon

1. _____
   _____
2. _____
   _____
3. _____
   _____
4. _____
   _____
5. _____
   _____
6. _____
   _____

I unleash my desire with love, trust and gratefulness.

Date:_____/_____/_____

Evening

1. _____
   _____
2. _____
   _____
3. _____
   _____
4. _____
   _____
5. _____
   _____
6. _____
   _____
7. _____
   _____
8. _____
   _____
9. _____
   _____

I unleash my desire with love, trust and gratefulness.

Date:_____/_____/_____

Morning

1. _____
   _____
2. _____
   _____
3. _____
   _____

Afternoon

1. _____
   _____
2. _____
   _____
3. _____
   _____
4 _____
   _____
5. _____
   _____
6. _____
   _____

I unleash my desire with love, trust and gratefulness.

Date:_____/_____/_____

Evening

1. _____
   _____

2. _____
   _____

3. _____
   _____

4 _____
   _____

5. _____
   _____

6. _____
   _____

7 _____
   _____

8. _____
   _____

9. _____
   _____

I unleash my desire with love, trust and gratefulness.

Date:_____/_____/_____

Morning

1. _____
   _____
2. _____
   _____
3. _____
   _____

Afternoon

1. _____
   _____
2. _____
   _____
3. _____
   _____
4 _____
   _____
5. _____
   _____
6. _____
   _____

I unleash my desire with love, trust and gratefulness.

Date:_____/_____/_____

Evening

1. _____
   _____
2. _____
   _____
3. _____
   _____
4 _____
   _____
5. _____
   _____
6. _____
   _____
7 _____
   _____
8. _____
   _____
9. _____
   _____

I unleash my desire with love, trust and gratefulness.

Date: _____ / _____ / _____

Morning

1. _____
   _____
2. _____
   _____
3. _____
   _____

Afternoon

1. _____
   _____
2. _____
   _____
3. _____
   _____
4 _____
   _____
5. _____
   _____
6. _____
   _____

I unleash my desire with love, trust and gratefulness.

Date:_____/_____/_____

Evening

1. _____
_____

2. _____
_____

3. _____
_____

4 _____
_____

5. _____
_____

6. _____
_____

7 _____
_____

8. _____
_____

9. _____
_____

I unleash my desire with love, trust and gratefulness.

Date:_____/_____/_____

Morning

1. _____
   _____
2. _____
   _____
3. _____
   _____

Afternoon

1. _____
   _____
2. _____
   _____
3. _____
   _____
4 _____
   _____
5. _____
   _____
6. _____
   _____

I unleash my desire with love, trust and gratefulness.

Date:_____/_____/_____

Evening

1. _____
   _____

2. _____
   _____

3. _____
   _____

4 _____
   _____

5. _____
   _____

6. _____
   _____

7 _____
   _____

8. _____
   _____

9. _____
   _____

I unleash my desire with love, trust and gratefulness.

Date:_____/_____/_____

Morning

1. _____
   _____
2. _____
   _____
3. _____
   _____

Afternoon

1. _____
   _____
2. _____
   _____
3. _____
   _____
4 _____
   _____
5. _____
   _____
6. _____
   _____

I unleash my desire with love, trust and gratefulness.

Date:_____/_____/_____

Evening

1. _____
   _____

2. _____
   _____

3. _____
   _____

4 _____
   _____

5. _____
   _____

6. _____
   _____

7 _____
   _____

8. _____
   _____

9. _____
   _____

I unleash my desire with love, trust and gratefulness.

Date:_____/_____/_____

Morning

1. _____
   _____
2. _____
   _____
3. _____
   _____

Afternoon

1. _____
   _____
2. _____
   _____
3. _____
   _____
4 _____
   _____
5. _____
   _____
6. _____
   _____

I unleash my desire with love, trust and gratefulness.

Date:_____/_____/_____
Evening

1. _____
   _____
2. _____
   _____
3. _____
   _____
4 _____
   _____
5. _____
   _____
6. _____
   _____
7 _____
   _____
8. _____
   _____
9. _____
   _____

I unleash my desire with love, trust and gratefulness.

Date:_____/_____/_____

Morning

1. _____
   _____
2. _____
   _____
3. _____
   _____

Afternoon

1. _____
   _____
2. _____
   _____
3. _____
   _____
4. _____
   _____
5. _____
   _____
6. _____
   _____

I unleash my desire with love, trust and gratefulness.

Date:_____/_____/_____

Evening

1. _____
   _____

2. _____
   _____

3. _____
   _____

4. _____
   _____

5. _____
   _____

6. _____
   _____

7. _____
   _____

8. _____
   _____

9. _____
   _____

I unleash my desire with love, trust and gratefulness.

Date:_____/_____/_____

Morning

1. _____
   _____
2. _____
   _____
3. _____
   _____

Afternoon

1. _____
   _____
2. _____
   _____
3. _____
   _____
4. _____
   _____
5. _____
   _____
6. _____
   _____

I unleash my desire with love, trust and gratefulness.

Date:_____/_____/_____

Evening

1. _____
   _____
2. _____
   _____
3. _____
   _____
4 _____
   _____
5. _____
   _____
6. _____
   _____
7 _____
   _____
8. _____
   _____
9. _____
   _____

I unleash my desire with love, trust and gratefulness.

Date:_____/_____/_____

Morning

1. _____
   _____
2. _____
   _____
3. _____
   _____

Afternoon

1. _____
   _____
2. _____
   _____
3. _____
   _____
4 _____
   _____
5. _____
   _____
6. _____
   _____

I unleash my desire with love, trust and gratefulness.

Date:_____/_____/_____
Evening

1. _____
_____

2. _____
_____

3. _____
_____

4 _____
_____

5. _____
_____

6. _____
_____

7 _____
_____

8. _____
_____

9. _____
_____

I unleash my desire with love, trust and gratefulness.

Date:_____/_____/_____

Morning

1. _____
   _____
2. _____
   _____
3. _____
   _____

Afternoon

1. _____
   _____
2. _____
   _____
3. _____
   _____
4 _____
   _____
5. _____
   _____
6. _____
   _____

I unleash my desire with love, trust and gratefulness.

Date:_____/_____/_____
Evening

1. _____
   _____
2. _____
   _____
3. _____
   _____
4 _____
   _____
5. _____
   _____
6. _____
   _____
7 _____
   _____
8. _____
   _____
9. _____
   _____

I unleash my desire with love, trust and gratefulness.

Date:_____/_____/_____

Morning

1. _____
   _____
2. _____
   _____
3. _____
   _____

Afternoon

1. _____
   _____
2. _____
   _____
3. _____
   _____
4. _____
   _____
5. _____
   _____
6. _____
   _____

I unleash my desire with love, trust and gratefulness.

Date:_____/_____/_____

Evening

1. _____
   _____

2. _____
   _____

3. _____
   _____

4 _____
   _____

5. _____
   _____

6. _____
   _____

7 _____
   _____

8. _____
   _____

9. _____
   _____

I unleash my desire with love, trust and gratefulness.

Date:_____/_____/_____

Morning

1. _____
   _____
2. _____
   _____
3. _____
   _____

Afternoon

1. _____
   _____
2. _____
   _____
3. _____
   _____
4 _____
   _____
5. _____
   _____
6. _____
   _____

I unleash my desire with love, trust and gratefulness.

Date:_____/_____/_____

Evening

1. _____
   _____
2. _____
   _____
3. _____
   _____
4 _____
   _____
5. _____
   _____
6. _____
   _____
7 _____
   _____
8. _____
   _____
9. _____
   _____

I unleash my desire with love, trust and gratefulness.

Date:_____/_____/_____

Morning

1. _____
   _____
2. _____
   _____
3. _____
   _____

Afternoon

1. _____
   _____
2. _____
   _____
3. _____
   _____
4 _____
   _____
5. _____
   _____
6. _____
   _____

I unleash my desire with love, trust and gratefulness.

Date:_____/_____/_____

Evening

1. _____
_____

2. _____
_____

3. _____
_____

4 _____
_____

5. _____
_____

6. _____
_____

7 _____
_____

8. _____
_____

9. _____
_____

I unleash my desire with love, trust and gratefulness.

Date:_____/_____/_____

Morning

1. _____
   _____
2. _____
   _____
3. _____
   _____

Afternoon

1. _____
   _____
2. _____
   _____
3. _____
   _____
4 _____
   _____
5. _____
   _____
6. _____
   _____

I unleash my desire with love, trust and gratefulness.

Date:_____/_____/_____
Evening

1. _____
_____
2. _____
_____
3. _____
_____
4 _____
_____
5. _____
_____
6. _____
_____
7 _____
_____
8. _____
_____
9. _____
_____

I unleash my desire with love, trust and gratefulness.

Date:_____/_____/_____

Morning

1. _____
   _____
2. _____
   _____
3. _____
   _____

Afternoon

1. _____
   _____
2. _____
   _____
3. _____
   _____
4. _____
   _____
5. _____
   _____
6. _____
   _____

I unleash my desire with love, trust and gratefulness.

Date:_____/_____/_____

Evening

1. _____
   _____

2. _____
   _____

3. _____
   _____

4. _____
   _____

5. _____
   _____

6. _____
   _____

7. _____
   _____

8. _____
   _____

9. _____
   _____

I unleash my desire with love, trust and gratefulness.

Date:_____/_____/_____

Morning

1. _____
   _____
2. _____
   _____
3. _____
   _____

Afternoon

1. _____
   _____
2. _____
   _____
3. _____
   _____
4 _____
   _____
5. _____
   _____
6. _____
   _____

I unleash my desire with love, trust and gratefulness.

Date:_____/_____/_____
Evening

1. _____
   _____
2. _____
   _____
3. _____
   _____
4 _____
   _____
5. _____
   _____
6. _____
   _____
7 _____
   _____
8. _____
   _____
9. _____
   _____

I unleash my desire with love, trust and gratefulness.

Date:_____/_____/_____

Morning

1. _____
   _____
2. _____
   _____
3. _____
   _____

Afternoon

1. _____
   _____
2. _____
   _____
3. _____
   _____
4 _____
   _____
5. _____
   _____
6. _____
   _____

I unleash my desire with love, trust and gratefulness.

Date:_____/_____/_____

Evening

1. _____
   _____
2. _____
   _____
3. _____
   _____
4 _____
   _____
5. _____
   _____
6. _____
   _____
7 _____
   _____
8. _____
   _____
9. _____
   _____

I unleash my desire with love, trust and gratefulness.

Date:_____/_____/_____

Morning

1. _____
   _____
2. _____
   _____
3. _____
   _____

Afternoon

1. _____
   _____
2. _____
   _____
3. _____
   _____
4 _____
   _____
5. _____
   _____
6. _____
   _____

I unleash my desire with love, trust and gratefulness.

Date:_____/_____/_____

Evening

1. _____
   _____
2. _____
   _____
3. _____
   _____
4 _____
   _____
5. _____
   _____
6. _____
   _____
7 _____
   _____
8. _____
   _____
9. _____
   _____

I unleash my desire with love, trust and gratefulness.

Date:_____/_____/_____

Morning

1. _____
   _____
2. _____
   _____
3. _____
   _____

Afternoon

1. _____
   _____
2. _____
   _____
3. _____
   _____
4 _____
   _____
5. _____
   _____
6. _____
   _____

I unleash my desire with love, trust and gratefulness.

Date:_____/_____/_____

Evening

1. _____
_____

2. _____
_____

3. _____
_____

4 _____
_____

5. _____
_____

6. _____
_____

7 _____
_____

8. _____
_____

9. _____
_____

I unleash my desire with love, trust and gratefulness.

Date:_____/_____/_____

Morning

1. _____
   _____
2. _____
   _____
3. _____
   _____

Afternoon

1. _____
   _____
2. _____
   _____
3. _____
   _____
4 _____
   _____
5. _____
   _____
6. _____
   _____

I unleash my desire with love, trust and gratefulness.

Date:_____/_____/_____

Evening

1. _____
_____
2. _____
_____
3. _____
_____
4 _____
_____
5. _____
_____
6. _____
_____
7 _____
_____
8. _____
_____
9. _____
_____

I unleash my desire with love, trust and gratefulness.

Date:_____/_____/_____

Morning

1. _____
   _____
2. _____
   _____
3. _____
   _____

Afternoon

1. _____
   _____
2. _____
   _____
3. _____
   _____
4 _____
   _____
5. _____
   _____
6. _____
   _____

I unleash my desire with love, trust and gratefulness.

Date:_____/_____/_____

Evening

1. _____
_____

2. _____
_____

3. _____
_____

4 _____
_____

5. _____
_____

6. _____
_____

7 _____
_____

8. _____
_____

9. _____
_____

I unleash my desire with love, trust and gratefulness.

Date:_____/_____/_____

Morning

1. _____
   _____
2. _____
   _____
3. _____
   _____

Afternoon

1. _____
   _____
2. _____
   _____
3. _____
   _____
4. _____
   _____
5. _____
   _____
6. _____
   _____

I unleash my desire with love, trust and gratefulness.

Date:_____/_____/_____

Evening

1. _____
   _____
2. _____
   _____
3. _____
   _____
4 _____
   _____
5. _____
   _____
6. _____
   _____
7 _____
   _____
8. _____
   _____
9. _____
   _____

I unleash my desire with love, trust and gratefulness.

Date:_____/_____/_____

Morning

1. _____
_____
2. _____
_____
3. _____
_____

Afternoon

1. _____
_____
2. _____
_____
3. _____
_____
4 _____
_____
5. _____
_____
6. _____
_____

I unleash my desire with love, trust and gratefulness.

Date:_____/_____/_____

Evening

1. _____

2. _____

3. _____

4 _____

5. _____

6. _____

7 _____

8. _____

9. _____

I unleash my desire with love, trust and gratefulness.

Date:_____/_____/_____

Morning

1. _____
   _____
2. _____
   _____
3. _____
   _____

Afternoon

1. _____
   _____
2. _____
   _____
3. _____
   _____
4 _____
   _____
5. _____
   _____
6. _____
   _____

I unleash my desire with love, trust and gratefulness.

Date:_____/_____/_____

Evening

1. _____
_____

2. _____
_____

3. _____
_____

4 _____
_____

5. _____
_____

6. _____
_____

7 _____
_____

8. _____
_____

9. _____
_____

I unleash my desire with love, trust and gratefulness.

Date:_____/_____/_____

Morning

1. _____
_____

2. _____
_____

3. _____
_____

Afternoon

1. _____
_____

2. _____
_____

3. _____
_____

4 _____
_____

5. _____
_____

6. _____
_____

I unleash my desire with love, trust and gratefulness.

Date:_____/_____/_____

Evening

1. _____
   _____

2. _____
   _____

3. _____
   _____

4 _____
   _____

5. _____
   _____

6. _____
   _____

7 _____
   _____

8. _____
   _____

9. _____
   _____

I unleash my desire with love, trust and gratefulness.

Date:_____/_____/_____

Morning

1. _____
   _____
2. _____
   _____
3. _____
   _____

Afternoon

1. _____
   _____
2. _____
   _____
3. _____
   _____
4 _____
   _____
5. _____
   _____
6. _____
   _____

I unleash my desire with love, trust and gratefulness.

Date:_____/_____/_____

Evening

1. _____
   _____
2. _____
   _____
3. _____
   _____
4 _____
   _____
5. _____
   _____
6. _____
   _____
7 _____
   _____
8. _____
   _____
9. _____
   _____

I unleash my desire with love, trust and gratefulness.

Date:_____/_____/_____

Morning

1. _____
   _____
2. _____
   _____
3. _____
   _____

Afternoon

1. _____
   _____
2. _____
   _____
3. _____
   _____
4 _____
   _____
5. _____
   _____
6. _____
   _____

I unleash my desire with love, trust and gratefulness.

Date:_____/_____/_____

Evening

1. _____
   _____

2. _____
   _____

3. _____
   _____

4 _____
   _____

5. _____
   _____

6. _____
   _____

7 _____
   _____

8. _____
   _____

9. _____
   _____

I unleash my desire with love, trust and gratefulness.

Date:_____/_____/_____

Morning

1. _____
_____
2. _____
_____
3. _____
_____

Afternoon

1. _____
_____
2. _____
_____
3. _____
_____
4 _____
_____
5. _____
_____
6. _____
_____

I unleash my desire with love, trust and gratefulness.

Date:_____/_____/_____

Evening

1. _____
   _____

2. _____
   _____

3. _____
   _____

4 _____
   _____

5. _____
   _____

6. _____
   _____

7 _____
   _____

8. _____
   _____

9. _____
   _____

I unleash my desire with love, trust and gratefulness.

Date:_____/_____/_____

Morning

1. _____
_____

2. _____
_____

3. _____
_____

Afternoon

1. _____
_____

2. _____
_____

3. _____
_____

4 _____
_____

5. _____
_____

6. _____
_____

I unleash my desire with love, trust and gratefulness.

Date:_____/_____/_____

Evening

1. _____
   _____

2. _____
   _____

3. _____
   _____

4 _____
   _____

5. _____
   _____

6. _____
   _____

7 _____
   _____

8. _____
   _____

9. _____
   _____

I unleash my desire with love, trust and gratefulness.

Date:_____/_____/_____

Morning

1. _____
   _____
2. _____
   _____
3. _____
   _____

Afternoon

1. _____
   _____
2. _____
   _____
3. _____
   _____
4 _____
   _____
5. _____
   _____
6. _____
   _____

I unleash my desire with love, trust and gratefulness.

Date:_____/_____/_____

Evening

1. _____
   _____

2. _____
   _____

3. _____
   _____

4 _____
   _____

5. _____
   _____

6. _____
   _____

7 _____
   _____

8. _____
   _____

9. _____
   _____

I unleash my desire with love, trust and gratefulness.

Made in the USA
Monee, IL
07 February 2022

90853361R00096